SEEDS
FOR THE
SPIRIT

Devotions for Spiritual Growth

Rev. Paul Simpson McElroy

**Wood Engraving by
Rik Olson**

PETER PAUPER PRESS, INC.
WHITE PLAINS • NEW YORK

Copyright © 1988 Peter Pauper Press, Inc.
ISBN 0-88088-485-1
Library of Congress No. 87-63107
Printed in the United States of America

Bible passages are from King James Version (KJV),
New International Version (NIV), Revised Standard
Version (RSV), The New American Bible (NAB), The
Jerusalem Bible (JB), The Living Bible (LB), The New
English Bible (NEB), Good News for Modern Man
(GN) and The New Testament in Modern English
(Phillips) (PME).

Devotions for Spiritual Growth
Listening to God

The Psalmist said: Wait on the Lord; be of good courage, and he shall strengthen thine heart; wait, I say, on the Lord. Psalm 27:14 (KJV) And James advised: *Draw near to God and he will draw near to you.* James 4:8 (RSV)

We often think of the profitable devotional period as one in which some problem has been solved, some new idea gained, or some intellectual stimulus received. There is value in such periods, but there are also values to be derived from a mind at rest, in just waiting quietly before the Lord. Our devotions and meditations are often so crowded with our own thoughts that we spend our time talking to God and we fail to let God talk to us.

At first even one minute of silence and stillness will seem empty and endless, but gradually these periods of quiet can be lengthened indefinitely, and soon periods of silent stillness will become alive and will be the most rewarding experiences of the day, as we discover how much God has to say to those who will listen. It is "in quietness and in confidence that we shall find our strength."

Clara Birkey has expressed this thought in these words:

> I built for Thee a quiet shrine
> Where oft I sit alone
> To wait for strength, or try to find
> The faith for going on.
>
> 'Tis there I sometimes say a prayer,
> Faint mumblings of my strife
> Or ponder long with greater minds
> The how and why of life.
>
> But only when I quiet wait,
> And wait in patience long,
> I find the strength I need
> The strength for going on.
>
> I find in Christ a way of life;
> I even find the sign,
> For while I wait in patience
> Comes: "Not my will, Lord, but Thine."

The purpose of devotional reading is not so much to expose our minds to new ideas or developments as to enter into a closer companionship with God. In devotional reading our whole being (not just our intellects) must be quieted, and made open, receptive, expectant, and above all else, humble.

Before reading the devotions that follow, try to relax and develop a quiet receptiveness in your whole person. Then, read a devotion (first the Scripture, then the author's reflection on the Scriptural passages, finally the Prayer), experience it fully, and let divine truths be revealed to you.

Draw nearer to God. Let God draw near to you.

P.S.M.

A Meditation on the Lord's Prayer

Our Father who art in heaven.
Creator and Very Source of all that is, who
came to earth in the form of man that we
might know and love Thee, grant that all
who call Thee Father may have the grace to
regard all Thy children as brothers.

Hallowed be Thy Name.
Help us to be so aware of what is true and
beautiful and good that day by day our lives
may show forth the beauty of Thy holiness.
Thou art holy; may Thy Name be hallowed
by us.

Thy kingdom come.
May we ever be ready to encourage that
which will make Thy kingdom more real to
others; re-assure us that the ideals of Jesus
are not far off dreams but a power that can
direct our lives here on earth.

*Thy will be done, on earth as it is in
heaven.*
May Thy will be done through us, for Thou
hast no hands but ours; no feet but ours; no
tongues but ours to do Thy will. May we
have a mind through which Thy Son, Christ,
thinks; a heart through which Christ loves; a

voice through which Christ speaks; and hands through which Christ helps. Not our will, but Thine, be done.

Give us this day our daily bread,
Enable us all to earn our daily living honestly without anxiety. Forbid that we accept benefits or gains at the expense of others.

And forgive us our debts as we
forgive our debtors.
We need Thy forgiveness. Lead us in Thy spirit to forgive our debtors.

Lead us not into temptation but
deliver us from evil.
Make clean our hearts within us that we may not be tempted by that which lowers. If we must go where Temptation is give us strength to withstand, for *Thine is the Kingdom and the Power and the Glory forever.*
Amen.

Religion Makes a Difference

If anyone considers himself religious and yet does not keep a tight rein on his tongue, he deceives himself and his religion is worthless. Religion that God our Father accepts as pure and faultless is this: to look after orphans and widows in their distress and to keep oneself from being polluted by the world. James 1:26-27 (NIV)

That there is a direct relationship between religion and good behavior, no one would deny. It usually follows that the genuinely religious person is also a person of so-called good behavior, although it does not always follow that the person of so-called good behavior is also a deeply religious person.

Religion is something more than good behavior. Religion is a point of view. It is not a way of looking at certain things, but a certain way of looking at all things. Religion is the tie that binds men and women to God and to all of humanity. It is the power that enables people to become what they should be, with a right approach to life. Religion is that process or means by which we keep in touch with the source from which all blessings flow.

People with a religious outlook are those who believe in a personal power, called God, with whom it is possible to commune. They believe in the ultimate triumph of righteousness, in the sacredness of human personality, and in the unlimited potentialities within every human being.

A person returning home from the Holy Land with a vial of water from the River Jordan discovered that in transit the water had grown foul and rancid. When removed from its source it had turned bad. So, too, we need to keep in touch with the Great Source of Life itself, and through religion we can. That is why religion makes a difference in life and in living.

Prayer:
Fashion my desires and deeds in accord with Your will that I may be instrumental in building a new world of righteousness. Give me a heart that is big enough, an imagination that is large enough and a strength that is great enough to meet the challenges I must face. Amen.

A Great Trust Is Ours

Don't fail to do these things that God entrusted to you. I Timothy 6:20 (LB) *From everyone who has been given much, much will be demanded; and from the one who has been entrusted with much, much more will be asked.* Luke 12:48 (NIV) *Whatever your task, work heartily, as serving the Lord and not men.* Colossians 3:23 (RSV)

It hurts to face the fact that we cannot blame God for our failure to perform tasks we should do ourselves. We are not impersonal marionettes pulled thither and yon by some omnipotent deity. We are human individuals endowed by God with freedom to choose what we want. But let us make sure that what we want is what God wants.

We are stewards who have received the gift of God's trust. Indeed, God is dependent upon us to proclaim to all the world that Jesus Christ is Lord. What a responsibility that is! What a treasure to be placed in such frail earthenware vessels as our human bodies. We are the instruments through which God must work to carry out divine plans.

Our failure to fulfill our tasks will hinder the kingdom by just so much. As Christians we have every right to expect great things from God and in turn God has every right to expect great things from us.

To attribute our actions to mere happenstance is like saying that the letters of the alphabet were blown together by a chance wind to form the great messages of the Bible. Surely, there is a mind behind the universe, there is purpose running through it, and there is meaning in it—and we are privileged to cooperate in the fulfillment of God's purpose.

Prayer:

Teach us, O God, that prayer is not fulfillment but preparation. O God, whom we hope to serve some other time, remind us how little time we have; tomorrow Thou has not given, only today. You have given us powers we seldom use and responsibilities we too readily relinquish. Enable us to see how much better we might be than we are. Amen.

A Right Spirit Within

If anyone wishes to be a follower of mine, he must leave self behind; he must take up his cross and come with me. Whoever cares for his own safety is lost; but if a man will let himself be lost for my sake, he will find his true self. What will a man gain by winning the whole world, at the cost of his true self? Or what can he give that will buy that self back?
Matthew 16:24-26 (NEB)

Persons with a right spirit within do not measure success in terms of whether their feeble strength and skill are a fair match for the opposing forces. They measure success in terms of whether or not they do their part in what ought to be done.

Such persons believe that righteousness will ultimately triumph, and willingly and sacrificially throw their weight, such as it is, with the side of moral rightness rather than with the side of expedience.

The person with a right spirit within will say in the face of danger and cruel opposition: "I may lose my life in the struggle that lies ahead, but I would rather

13

lose my life fighting for a cause in which I believe than live a life which lacks all meaning."

Without a shadow of doubt God orders our doings better than we could have planned for ourselves. That is why it is good to let God speak in and through us. When that happens our sense of values changes and we let what is called the Christian spirit govern our actions. Strive to have that mind in you which was in Christ Jesus.

Prayer:
O God, I know I cannot live as I want unless my wants are in accord with yours. Give me the desire and the strength to live this day as I ought. Amen.

Learning to be Content

*And I am not saying this because I feel neglected;
for I have learned to be satisfied with what I have. I
know what it is to be in need, and what it is to have
more than enough. I have learned this secret, so that
anywhere, at any time, I am content, whether I am
full or hungry, whether I have too much or too little.
I have the strength to face all conditions by the
power that Christ gives me.* Philippians 4:11-13
(GN)

Saint Paul maintained that no matter how
serious difficulties may be, it is possible to
endure them with a quality of spirit which
has been translated as "being content." By
this he did not mean that he was satisfied
with life. He was not a fatalist accepting
everything that happened as being for the
best and therefore not to be challenged or
left unchanged.

When Paul tells us how he had learned
under all conditions of life to be self-
sufficient, he takes care to add that he does
not rely wholly on himself. He is conscious
of what he calls the inward power of Christ,

who at all times supplies him with the needed strength.

Jesus assured his followers that they could not endure all trials and tribulations by their own strength. Our problems are too great, more than is humanly possible to endure by ourselves. All human effort must forever be futile unless it is aided by the power of Christ.

We have within us that which is divine. God made us in God's own image, a little lower than the angels. To live in that consciousness is to be able to call into service a power that will help. It is a case of learning to put our trust, our confidence, in God rather than in worldly, material power. "Be not dismayed whate'er betide, God will take care of you."

Prayer:

O God, in times of adversity help me to keep my perspective and inward poise. Enable me to endure hardships, even injustices, without complaint and without retaliation. May your love be a healing balm, uniting me to all humankind. Amen.

To Withstand or Submit?

Do everything possible, on your part, to live at peace with all men. Romans 12:18 (GN) *Judge not, that you be not judged.* Matthew 7:1 (RSV) *Bless those who persecute you; bless and do not curse them. Rejoice with those who rejoice, weep with those who weep. Live in harmony with one another.* Romans 12:14-16 (RSV)

God has created us to live not as hermits but as brothers and sisters, one to another. We are all children of God. Life, then, becomes a matter of relationships. We must therefore live in harmony and concord with our fellows or else be at enmity with them and separated from each other. Differences of opinion are a natural by-product of our God-given right to freedom of choice and freedom of will.

How then can we get along with those with whom we will inevitably differ and whose rights impinge upon what we believe to be our rights?

To submit to the demands of others is not always weakness. There may be more to be gained ultimately by yielding and thereby preserving harmony and cooperation than by adamantly opposing the wishes of others and thereby alienating them. We may discover healing powers through cooperation that are not available to those who insist upon having their own way.

Over and above this method of resolving differences is that of commitment to Jesus Christ. If we would try to please the Lord Jesus Christ instead of ourselves, much of our friction and many of our problems would vanish.

The secret is to test our actions by what we believe Jesus Himself would have us do, and this involves a study of Jesus in depth.

Prayer:
Dear Lord, Creator of all mankind, make me a channel through which Thy divine love may reach the lives of some of those who are near to me. Give me a heart sensitive to the needs of those with whom I may differ. Amen.

Our Opportunity

By the grace God gave me, I succeeded as an architect and laid the foundations, on which someone else is doing the building. I Corinthians 3:10 (JB) *The Spirit of God joins with our spirit in testifying that we are God's children; and if children, then, heirs. We are God's heirs and Christ's fellow-heirs. . . .* Romans 8:16-17 (NEB) *God created man in his own image, in the image of God created he him; male and female created he them.* Genesis 1:27 (KJV)

In "The Last Voyage," Alfred Noyes tells of a little girl who was taken ill on board ship in mid-Atlantic. After examining the child the ship's physician determined that he couldn't save her but that Dr. Marlowe at Johns Hopkins might. Dr. Marlowe was somewhere on the Atlantic, and soon, a tiny spark pierced the wide darkness of the howling sea and the two doctors were in communication. Dr. Marlowe advised to operate.

One fellow passenger hearing the news remarked to another, "You think they'll save her?" "Yes," came the reply, "they may save her, but who are *they?*"

Was it the ship's surgeon, Dr. Marlowe,

the radio operator, the captain? Yes, in part, but it was also a host of known and unknown down through the ages who had helped perfect medical science, nautical science, and wireless. Thousands of people had worked together to make possible that successful operation in mid-Atlantic.

To be one of thousands who are working together to help make possible some worthy event in our day—that is our opportunity!

The part we play in the Great Design may be inconspicuous, but it may nevertheless be essential to the fulfillment of the kingdom. God depends upon us and that need is our opportunity to do what we can in cooperation with others, however little it may be, to the glory of God. Inasmuch as we do anything unto one of the least of God's children, we do it unto Him.

Prayer:
O God, the Creator of us all, make us mindful of our indebtedness to the host of known and unknown who have enriched our lives, and grant that we may be aware of our opportunity to be one of many working together toward the fulfillment of Your kingdom.
Amen.

Strength to Overcome

[The Lord said:] *"My grace is enough for you: for where there is weakness, my power is shown the more completely." Therefore, I have cheerfully made up my mind to be proud of my weaknesses, because they mean a deeper experience of the power of Christ. I can even enjoy weaknesses, insults, privations, persecutions and difficulties for Christ's sake. For my very weakness makes me strong in him.* II Corinthians 12:9-10 (PME)

At some time in life most of us have to face adversity in one form or other, whether a simple inconvenience or a major tragedy. Misfortunes may represent setbacks, but they need not mean failure. It is not what happens to us, but how we react, that is important. What we deem a handicap may prove to be an asset or an opportunity.

Yachtsmen know that the wind seldom blows from the direction that will carry them straight to their destination, and thus they have to tack or zig-zag back and forth across the course. So, too, the Chinese Checkers player knows that it may be necessary to move sideways in order to go forward.

Sometimes we have our hearts set on the wrong thing, and our misfortune may be the very means of making possible what could not otherwise be achieved. This unknown author found his handicaps to be assets:

I asked for strength that I might
    achieve, I was made weak that I
    might obey;
I asked for health that I might do
    greater things, I was given sickness
    that I might do better things;
I asked for riches that I might be
    happy, I was given poverty that I
    might be wise;
I asked for power that I might serve my
    fellowmen, I was given weakness that
    I might feel the need of God.
I was given nothing I asked for—all that
    I hoped for; my prayer was
    answered—I was most blessed.

Prayer:
I thank Thee for the power to overcome my misfortunes, to learn from what life gives me. Amen.

About Prayer

Let the words of my mouth, and the meditation of my heart, be acceptable in thy sight, O Lord, my strength and my redeemer. Psalm 19:14 (KJV)
Search me, O God, and know my heart: try me, and know my thoughts: And see if there be any wicked way in me, and lead me in the way everlasting. Psalm 139:23-24 (KJV)

Prayer is not an attempt to get what we want, but an endeavor to give God an opportunity to do what God wants through us. Prayer is not begging from God, but cooperating with God. The thing to be sought is not how to get our way, but how to accept the will of God. The intent is not to change God, but to change ourselves; not to try to change God's mind, but to change our attitudes.

Prayer is really thinking in God's presence. As the level of our consciousness is raised toward the level of God's thoughts, the happenings of life are seen in true perspective. Effective prayer involves a deep yearning to know God, an eagerness to trust God all the way, an ability to relinquish our hold, and a willingness to let go and let God.

Prayer assumes that there is a God—a Spirit, a Power, a Force—that created the universe, and that this creating process is still going on under God's guidance. It assumes that God is available and interested in the welfare of every one of us, and that it is possible for us to commune with God.

A habit of regular prayer will make life noticeably changed. It will afford an equanimity of spirit and a greater concern for others. Prayer can turn one from that which is wrong toward that which is right. It can put one in touch with God.

Prayer:

O God whose hand is evident in the immensity of the heavens and in the most minute particles of the earth, in galaxies and in atoms, whose wonders are revealed through telescope and microscope, whose power is evident in the wind, the storm and the calm, and whose love is known to all, I praise your glorious name and I come believing you will hear my prayers. Amen.

A View of Life

There is no man that hath power over the spirit to retain the spirit; neither hath he power in the day of death. Ecclesiastes 8:8 (KJV) *For this perishable nature of ours must be wrapped in imperishability, these bodies which are mortal must be wrapped in immortality.* I Corinthians 15:53 (PME) *The Lord is my shepherd; I shall not want . . . . Yea, though I walk through the valley of the shadow of death, I will fear no evil: for thou art with me . . . .* Psalm 23:1, 4 (KJV)

A friend once wrote: "I wish so much that people could be made to consider their bodies in what, it seems to me, is the proper relation to their real selves. I refuse to believe that my body is myself. It is only the house I live in, and anything that happens to it does not happen to me. If our material house is damaged by wind, fire, or just by the ravages of time, we are made uncomfortable, as we have to live in it, and so we like to keep it in as good a state of repair as possible."

He continued: "That line of thought has

been a great comfort to me in regard to death. I absolutely believe that when that event takes place, still nothing has happened to the real person I knew and loved. He or she has just slipped out of that 'house' leaving it looking just as it did, but empty as any physical house is when the occupants have moved. And how different an empty house seems! We walk through rooms which may look the same with furniture unchanged, etc., and yet we feel so different, for it all seems so empty, but really lacking only the personality which for us gave it life."

Prayer:
O God, I thank Thee for giving me those whom I have known and loved, and who have meant as much to me as they have. Help me to think of death as not the end but the beginning of a life that shall transcend my highest hopes. For those who have made the distant heavens a home for me and whose truth and beauty are even now in my heart, I thank Thee, Lord. Amen.

As Christians

*Jesus of Nazareth . . . was a prophet, powerful in
word and deed before God and all the people.* Luke
24:19 (NIV) *Anyone who wants to follow me must
put aside his own desires and conveniences and
carry his cross with him every day and keep close to
me!* Luke 9:23 (LB)

A contemporary of the First Century
Christians said that "with them temperance
dwells, self-restraint is practiced, monogamy
is observed, chastity is guarded, inequity
exterminated, sin extirpated, righteousness
exercised, law administered, worship per-
formed, and God acknowledged." This is
made possible, said he, "because with them
truth governs their actions, grace guards
them, the Bible guides them, wisdom
teaches them, and God reigns in their
hearts." Could this be said of modern
Christians?

The secret of attaining such conduct is to
take care always to place before our eyes the
sole pleasure of God.

James Russell Lowell once challenged the
skeptics to find a place ten miles square on

29

the globe where a man could live in comfort, security and decency, where he could find education for his children, reverence for infancy and old age, honor for womanhood, or any sacred regard for human life, where the gospel of Christ had not gone before and cleared the way, laying a foundation for such conditions of affairs. Such is the power of the gospel.

The secret of this transforming power which Christians profess obliges them to believe that God sees them day and night, penetrates their secret thoughts. From this proceeds their great reverence for God's sovereign majesty, and their great fear of offending God.

Prayer:

God, may the need of the world for charity and commitment be the need that speaks to us. Grant that we may be worthy of the vocation to which we have been called. May we, as Christians, never lose sight of the needs of the world that we are called to meet, and may we always be assured of Thy presence and power as we respond to the activities of each day. Amen.

The Demands of Religion

Do not merely listen to the word, and so deceive yourselves. Do what it says. Anyone who listens to the word but does not do what it says is like a man who looks at his face in a mirror . . . James 1:22-23 (NIV) *Therefore you have no excuse, O man, whoever you are, when you judge another; for in passing judgment upon him you condemn yourself, because you, the judge, are doing the very same things.* Romans 2:1 (RSV)

What is religion all about?

Religion is about life, about how to live it, and how to take it. Religion is the tie that binds us to God, to ourselves, and to other people. Religion is not a thing apart from life, it is life itself, lived at its very best.

To be sure, religion places certain claims or obligations upon us. As sincerely religious persons we cannot do certain things that others do. For instance, we cannot advance ourselves at the expense of others; we cannot speak unkindly of others; we cannot take all we want for ourselves when others must go without.

It is also true that religious people must

do certain things, such as go the second mile, do justly, show mercy, and walk humbly with God.

Religion does make a difference in our outlook, in our viewpoint, in our sense of values.

Religion is also very practical. A religion that does nothing, that gives nothing, that costs nothing, that suffers nothing, is worth nothing.

Prayer:
There are needs in the world, O Lord, of which we are unaware. There are needs which we know about, but which are beyond our powers to meet. We cannot do much but we can do something and we would resolve right now to do what we can. When our strength is added to Thine, then naught else matters, for "with Thee all things are possible." Amen.

A Meditation: The Hand of God

Years ago, when it was discovered that a total eclipse of the moon would appear in Cairo, Egypt, some of the teachers of the American University at Cairo decided to visit one of the villages on the outskirts of the city to observe the reactions of the people there who, lacking newspapers or radio, knew nothing of the coming eclipse.

As the shadow began to creep across the moon, the teachers asked a villager what was happening. Nonchalantly, he replied: "Oh, that is just the moon hiding behind a mountain." Another said that a cloud was covering the moon. Then, at the time of the total eclipse, the question was put to the village elder who, with imagination, replied, "Friends, don't be alarmed. This is just the hand of God covering the moon."

Would that we in our dark hours might see the hand of God at work in our lives, and in the world about us. Amen.

Values in Meditation

Try hard to make yourself worthy of God's approval, a workman who has no cause to be ashamed, following a straight course in preaching the truth. II Timothy 2:15 (NAB) *In quietness and trust is your strength.* Isaiah 30:15 (NIV) *Wait on the Lord; be of good courage, and he shall strengthen thine heart; wait, I say, on the Lord.* Psalm 27:14 (KJV) *They that wait upon the Lord shall renew their strength.* Isaiah 40:31 (KJV)

Moments of meditation may seem to the uninitiated as idle, daydreaming, and a waste of time. True, these minutes may seem unproductive and of no apparent value, but character is not made only in the grand and exciting events of life. It is also through constant, daily moments spent quietly with God that many a person has found the faith for going on.

People accustomed to daily devotions may not be spared from doing wrong, but little by little, day by day, they can through meditation build into themselves a viewpoint, an attitude, a character that is reflected in their conduct.

Jesus urged his disciples to come apart and rest a while, to withdraw from society, and pray. Time spent in such reflection, in pondering on the meaning of life, in seeking ways to make the teachings and spirit of the Master more meaningful, is an investment.

Only in this way can the indispensable and abiding values of life become a vital part of our being. The saints found that it takes time to be holy.

𝔓rayer:

In the quiet of these moments help us, O God, to find quiet for our souls. For we need quietness. In Thy presence, there is quietness. O God, let us find Thy presence now. Let us be still that we may know that Thou art God. Amen.

A Meditation: Within Our Lifetime

Within the span of our lifetimes, we and all the others of our generation hold in our hands all that is of value from past civilizations, and in those same hands we hold the hope of all that is to come.

We are, so to speak, the living link between the ageless past and the timeless future. We are poised, if but for the brief span of a lifetime, amid eternity. In that time it is our duty to hold sacred within ourselves all that is of value from the past and to pass on the best from that past toward the building of the best that is to be.

Only as the good of the past can pass through us will the future of civilization be safeguarded.

We cannot be responsible for everything. It is true that around each of us is drawn a fatal circle beyond which we cannot pass, but within that circle we are powerful and free. Let us remember that to that extent we are responsible trustees of the future.

Let us meditate on that circle which defines us, that sphere of our potential action. Let us feel our hearts and minds grow to fill that circle with love, selflessness, and devotion. Let the possibilities of positive personal action become apparent to us. Amen.

A Good Example

Never pay back evil for evil. Romans 12:17 (LB)
*Love each other with brotherly affection and take
delight in honoring each other.* Romans 12:10
(LB) *We who are strong ought to bear with the
failings of the weak.* Romans 15:1 (RSV)

The example of a good life is one of the
most powerful influences for good in the
world. People who constantly strive to bend
their efforts in the direction of the good life,
even though they err at times, will be an
inspiration to others. Even when we are
motivated by a desire to do what is right, we
may be guilty of mistakes, but they will more
likely be mistakes of judgment than mistakes
of intent or spirit.

To aim at righteousness, justice, good
behavior, and honor will more likely bring
good results than if such goals are ignored.
A conscientious follower of Christ will be of
a reputable character, and knows to choose a
good name even over great wealth. A
Christian tries to see God in people, in
events, in actions, and tries to discover the

truth as it is, and to live accordingly, even if it hurts.

People with hearts that are pure and purposes that are noble will find an extra strength within themselves. Their strength will be as the strength of tens because their hearts are pure.

To live a good life requires what is called grace, that is, the doing for another kindnesses he doesn't deserve, hasn't earned, could not ask for, and can't repay. Grace offers to a person what he cannot do for himself.

Prayer:
Our Father, if we have neglected our duties, if we have let someone down who is dependent upon us, if we have uttered unkind words or entertained mean thoughts, forgive us, and instill in us such love and loyalty toward Thee that we will truly be instruments through which Thy will is done. Amen.

The Relevance of Jesus

Jesus answered, "I am the way—and the truth and the life. No one comes to the Father except through me." John 14:6 (NIV) *"Come to me, all you who are weary and burdened, and I will give you rest."* Matthew 11:28 (NIV) *Simon Peter answered and said, Thou art the Christ, the Son of the living God.* Matthew 16:16 (KJV)

Our regard for Jesus affects every act and decision that we make and it determines the faith we live by. Many people who call themselves "Christian" may have very little understanding or appreciation of Jesus. A little knowledge of Jesus is not just a personal loss; it is a dangerous thing.

People who acknowledge the authority of Jesus in their lives may reasonably expect to have light thrown upon their actions and decisions. We are saved by our beliefs just as surely as we are ruined by our beliefs. Unless we are buttressed from within by strong Christian convictions we are the more vulnerable to un-Christian or anti-Christian doctrines.

Jesus' personality, teachings and example

are such that he still influences the world today. From Jesus people can learn a philosophy of life, a guide for living. Jesus remains relevant because of his ability to make people better persons than they now are.

Jesus has given us truths which must be followed by all, whether they label themselves Christians or not. He has shown us how to live. The world cannot ignore Jesus and long survive, for his teachings, example, and spirit represent the very foundations on which society exists.

Prayer:
Almighty God, the Father of our Lord Jesus Christ, forgive us those things whereof our conscience is afraid, and give us those good things which we are not worthy to ask, but through the merits and mediation of Jesus Christ, Thy Son, our Lord. Amen.

Today's Opportunities

As we have opportunity, let us do good to all people.
Galatians 6:10 (NIV) *So don't be anxious about
tomorrow. God will take care of your tomorrow too.
Live one day at a time.* Matthew 6:34 (LB)

Thank God every morning when you get up
that you have something to do which must
be done, whether you like it or not. Being
forced to work, and forced to do your best,
will breed in you temperance, self-control,
diligence, strength of will, contentment, and
a hundred other virtues which the idle will
never know. For the needs of the world
which you alone can meet, be grateful.

No man or woman, even of the humblest
sort, can really be strong, gentle, pure and
good without the world being better for it,
without somebody being helped and
comforted by the very existence of that
goodness.

"Today, do all the good you can, by all the
means you can, in all the ways you can, in all
the places you can, all the times you can, to
all the people you can, as long as ever you
can," advised John Wesley.

Never put off until tomorrow what you can do today. The standard which Jesus set for himself might well be applied to us: "We must work the works of him who sent me, while it is day; night comes, when no one can work." *John 9:4 (RSV)* Today's opportunity to witness for the Lord may be lost, if postponed until tomorrow.

Prayer:
O Lord, for the opportunities of this day to render service to others, to express joy, to witness to Thee, I am grateful. Don't allow me to let these opportunities pass, unheeded. Amen.

Each Thing Important

Consecrate yourselves today to the Lord. Exodus
32:29 (KJV) *In order that none of you be deceived
by sin and become stubborn, you must help one
another every day, as long as the "Today" in the
scripture applies to us.* Hebrews 3:13 (GN)

Just as our today has been determined by
the way we lived yesterday, so our tomorrow
is determined by the way we live today. We
are not at liberty to act as freely and
independently as we choose because we are
conditioned by our past. Our character, for
instance, is determined largely by the
decisions we make for ourselves, and those
decisions will govern the decisions we make
today for tomorrow. You can never tell when
you do an act just what the result will be.

We cannot always see the results of the
things we try to do. Our acts, like arrows
shot into the air, may fall we know not
where. Our deeds, our lives, may seemingly
count for little, but like the locusts who
come to the water's edge and are swept
away, they may count for much. The locusts'

49

dead bodies may form a bridge over which others may cross. So too, our lives today may become the foundation on which others will build tomorrow. To the extent that we, directly or indirectly, influence history we are the instruments of destiny. Who knows but we were born for just such a time as this?

Our little deeds of kindliness oft fall on uncongenial ground, yet only as we cool this heated earth with our myriad deeds of lovingness can we convert a land of earthly sinners into God's great kingdom of love and worth.

Prayer:
O God, Creator, Friend, we come before You feeling there is so much to be done that we despair of finishing our day's work. May we be as confident that You will be with us in the days ahead as we know You have been with us in the past. Take us and use us in Your service. Amen.

A Teaching: The Difference Between Heaven and Hell

According to an old fable, there once was a man who remarked that he did not know whether he would prefer to spend eternity in heaven or in hell. "Judging from what I have found of both places," he said, "neither appeals to me very much."

Instantly his friend was transformed into an angel. "How would you like to visit hell?" the angel asked. The man said that he was agreeable to a short visit if he could also take a quick look at heaven, so that he could compare the two.

"Agreed," said the angel, and, presto, they were transported to the nether regions. There before them was a banquet room with long tables piled high with delectable food. But the people around the tables were writhing in frustration because their arms were encased in splints so that they could not bend their elbows to lift the food to their mouths.

The man begged to be taken away as

quickly as possible to heaven.

To his surprise, heaven looked very much the same—a banquet room, tables laden with food, and people seated around the tables. They too could not bend their arms, for their elbows were encased in splints.

"Now," the angel asked, "do you see the difference?" "Yes," the man replied, the people in heaven are feeding each other."

Prayer:
Lord, O Source of Life, help us to make this earth a heaven and not a hell, through daily acts of cooperation and unselfishness. Amen.

A Brave Soul

Greater love hath no man than this, that a man lay down his life for his friends. John 15:13 (KJV)

One day in Queenstown, New Zealand, the author and his wife went for a walk through a magnificent park on the banks of Lake Wakatipu. It was a peaceful setting amid brilliantly colored flower beds and giant redwood trees. Suddenly a sole boulder loomed ahead, so immense that it seemed out of place geologically. On this gigantic boulder the following words could be discerned:

> "To commemorate the patient, stubborn invincible courage, the loyal comradeship, and brilliant achievement of Cap't. Lawrence E. G. Oates, Lieutenant Henry Bowers and Petty Officer Edgar Evans who reached the South Pole 17 January 1912 and perished on the return journey."

Nearby in bronze were these words from

Scott's diary telling of the last days of the expedition and describing Cap't. Oates:

"He was a brave soul. He slept through the night, hoping not to wake, but awoke in the morning. It was blowing blizzard. Oates said 'I am just going outside and I may be some time.' He went into the blizzard and we have not seen him since."

Oates realized that he could march no more and that his comrades would not willingly leave him. By going out to meet death, he left them free to push on to take the chance of life that remained to them.

Prayer:
Lord, help me to be a brave soul, to give sacrificially of myself. Let me lead my life so as to enhance and enrich the lives of others. Amen.

Asking for Trouble

Whenever you have to face trials of many kinds,
count yourselves supremely happy, in the knowledge
that such testing of your faith breeds fortitude, and if
you give fortitude full play you will go on to complete
a balanced character that will fall short in nothing.
James 1:1-4 (NEB)

It is natural for us to want to avoid trouble.
We shy away, understandably so, from
situations that are likely to cause us pain or
inconvenience. We feel that disturbances
create lots of extra work without accom-
plishing much constructively. It seems just
good common sense to try to stay out of
trouble.

There are, however, positive values in
dealing with trouble, values which would not
be available otherwise. Helen Keller said: "I
thank God for my handicaps, for through
them I have found myself, my work, and my
God." Out of trial, trouble, and tribulation
come experience, judgment, and strength.

Alice James, the sister of her famous
brothers William and Henry, was an invalid
most of her life, but her biographer said of

her, "She never accepted the horizon of invalidism." It is not the trouble that counts; it is the way in which we cope with that trouble.

Perhaps the darkest day of Christopher Columbus' voyage of discovery to the New World was when his three small ships were tossed about by a heavy storm, all three being damaged and the Pinta losing its rudder. The crews threatened mutiny on that dark day, and boldly told Columbus they would throw him overboard if he did not turn back. They were desperate and in dead earnest.

At the end of that day, Columbus wrote only five words in his log. They were: "This day we sailed on."

Prayer:
O Lord, help me to remain firm in my trust in You in times of adversity, and to learn and grow strong from my trials. Wrap me in the folds of Your strength and each day, together, we will sail on. Amen.

Living with Others

One man helps another, one says to the other, "Keep on!" The craftsman encourages the goldsmith, the one who beats with the hammer, him who strikes on the anvil; he says the soldering is good, and he fastens it with nails to steady it. Isaiah 41:6-7 (NAB)

In the world in which we live we must mingle with people whose manners and mannerisms annoy us, whose habits and practices offend us, and whose ideas and beliefs disturb us. Somehow, we must learn to get along with these people, or else be forever at odds with them, with ourselves, and with God.

How may we establish wholesome relationships with others?

First, we must recognize that no matter what minority interests we ourselves may represent we are, as are others, all at the same time members of a larger society whose more inclusive loyalties must be preserved. The part is never greater than the whole.

Second, we should ask: "Do our plans tend to separate us from common interests?" We must try to supplant jealousies and hatred with love. Hate separates; love unites.

Third, let us not force others to accept our viewpoints, but rather let the things for which we stand win their way into the hearts of others through their inherent goodness and merit.

Fourth, we should not only try to see things from others' viewpoints, but we should also try to see things from God's viewpoint.

Fifth, we could profit from the teachings, the example, and the spirit of Jesus and so discover, as did he, a love that is strong enough to transcend petty differences. "Let us love one another."

𝔓rayer:
As the rays of the sun fall alike on black and white, on Jew and Gentile, on Oriental and Occidental, so may all men and women come to look to Thee as the source of all their light and power, and upon Thy Son, Jesus Christ, as the light of the world. Amen. (See Colossians 3:11.)

Everything Is Important

If we put bits into the mouths of horses that they may obey us, we guide their whole bodies. Look at the ships also; though they are so great and are driven by strong winds, they are guided by a very small rudder wherever the will of the pilot directs. So the tongue is a little member and boasts of great things. How great a forest is set ablaze by a small fire! James 3:3-5 (RSV)

To the stonecutter hammering at rock, a hundred blows of hammer on chisel may make no apparent difference, yet the one hundred and first blow may split the rock in two. It is, of course, not just the last blow that fractures the stone but the cumulative effect of all the blows that have gone before. Every one of them counts!

One blow, one deed, one word, one minute, or one decision in itself may seem small and inconsequential, yet every one counts. Someone has said that character is the sum total of decisions one makes for oneself. An unknown author has expressed the same thought in these words:

A snowflake is so very small,
We scarcely think of it at all;
And yet, enough of them will make
A barrier we cannot break . . . .
A word is but a breath of air
'Tis heard or spoken without care;
Yet words in fierce profusion hurled
Upset the history of the world.

Big things are made up of little things, and
important events are made possible by
seemingly unimportant little things.

Every effort on our part, however feeble it
may seem, helps or hinders progress by just
so much. Nothing is too small in God's
sight. High motives and human need make
small deeds great.

Prayer:
*Source of all mankind, who sends the rain upon the
just and the unjust, and whose Son has taught that
You rejoice more over one lost sheep that is found
than over ninety and nine which went not astray,
give me a heart sensitive to the needs of those whose
lives afford less hope and joy than mine. Amen.*

A Prayer: Thou Who Art Good and Holy

You may ask me for anything in my name, and I will do it. John 14:14 (NIV) *Search me, O God, and know my heart; test me and know my anxious thoughts. See if there is any offensive way in me, and lead me in the way everlasting.* Psalm 139:23-24 (NIV)

O Thou who art perfect and holy, above and beyond all else, I come to worship Thee. I am awed by Thy power yet attracted by Thy goodness. My behavior falls so far short of Thy demands or Thy righteousness, and my achievements fall so far short of the standards and example Thou hast set before me, that I am afraid to come before Thee, yet I dare to come only because I need Thee.

I marvel at the beauty and orderliness and the vastness of Thy creations. I marvel at Thy patience with my impatience. I marvel at Thy forgiveness of my intolerance. I marvel at Thy understanding of my sinfulness. Only because Thy steadfast love is great enough to embrace me can I, errant and undeserving as I am, come into Thy presence.

I ask for wisdom to see things as they are. Help me to realize that Thou dost often chasten those whom Thou dost love. Forbid that I regard peace and the absence of conflict as the fulfillment of Thy will. Help me to see that peace and calm may be but indifference or temporary suppression of evil. Let me not think of the granting of my wishes as an assurance that I am right. Help me to see that only that is right which is in accord with Thy will.

This prayer I offer in the name of and for the sake of Him whom I love and seek to serve, even Jesus Christ. Amen.

Biographical Note

Reverend Paul Simpson McElroy is the retired minister of the First Congregational Church of St. Louis. Prior to being called to St. Louis, he had ministries in Providence, Rhode Island, and in Danvers and Manchester, Massachusetts. For over five years he contributed to the St. Louis Globe-Democrat a column entitled "Live a Little More." Among his books published by Peter Pauper Press are Inspiration for Living, Life's Wondrous Ways, Live a Little More, The Meditations of My Heart, Moments of Meditation, Prayers & Graces of Thanksgiving, Quiet Thoughts, Wisdom of the Bible, and Words of Comfort. *Reverend McElroy and his wife Clara have two daughters and five grandchildren. He was the first American to climb Mount Kilimanjaro.*